LEN'S ROAD TAKEN

Or

Building a Company and People

LEN'S ROAD TAKEN

BY

LEONARD GILMAN

www.bookstandpublishing.com

Published by
Bookstand Publishing
Morgan Hill, CA 95037
4781_7

ISBN 978-1-63498-940-4

CONTENTS

MILES LUMBER COMPANY

It began in 1955. I was twenty-six years old. I was working for Hy Spector selling shoes in his various department store concessions in and around Boston. My parents had gone on a South America cruise and had befriended a younger couple from Minneapolis. Miles and Shirley seemed to regard Herman and Anne as surrogate parents and at each island they took excursions together. By the end of the cruise my father was talking to them as if they were beloved children. When they got home from that cruise my father told me there was a man in Minneapolis he wanted me to meet.

Miles Fiterman was young (perhaps in his late 30's) and was a free spender. Dad said Miles was in the business of selling pre-cut garages and if I was interested he would be glad to spend several days showing me all the facets of that business. My father and I flew to Minneapolis. Dad stayed for only an overnight, and I shadowed Miles for close to a week. He explained how he arranged for the financing of a home improvement with the FHA and how to estimate the necessary concrete yardage and its cost for the garage slab.

What neither of us took into consideration was the fact that in Minnesota the land was as flat as a pancake and was all easy to dig soil. In New England most all the land had a slope and in what I was eventually reminded of was that the presence of ledge was commonplace. Miles agreed I would run an ad for Gilman Pre-Cut Garages with a coupon attached. He would fly out to go with me on a few sales calls and we would form a business partnership as equal partners. Miles flew into Boston for the purpose of going with me in response to the mail in coupons included in the garage ads I placed.

The response was poor and Miles decided it wasn't going to be a good business in hilly New England. I enjoyed being outdoors more than sniffing feet in the shoe store, and was determined to make a go of it.

The company's first advertisement – 1955.

My father staked me to the cost of my first few newspaper display ads in the Boston Globe, Herald and Post. He invested $500 in me and my venture. That was it. I never went back for more.

I hired Sal Bordeiri a local mason. He and I would drag and then float the wet Redi-Mix concrete for the slab of the first garage I sold. That first year in business I learned everything I had to know from Sal about pouring garage slabs, and particularly how many cubic yards to order, and by the second year in business I knew the dispatchers by name and how to compute time for delivery, etc. In those days I paid $13.50 per cubic yard of Redi-mix concrete. I checked and now, in 2020, a cubic yard of Redi-Mix concrete costs $147. As I write, I doubt you really care about the price of concrete in 1955, just sit back, scroll thru my 'story' and bear with me. There will not be a test at the end.

79 MILK STREET, BOSTON

My first year in business I operated as Gilman Garage Inc. I had a desk in my father's office on Milk Street across from Boston's Chinatown. Dad shared the office with his accountant and best friend Barney Yanofsky. It would take pages to explain why Barney remains in my mind all these years as the "Most Unforgettable and Interesting Man I Ever Met". Barney (everyone always referred to him as "BY") had an interest in a ticket agency, and for 'sold-out' any sporting event or hit play he could always get me tickets. One time in the early 70's I had to stay alone in Boston recuperating after a hospital stay. We had already moved to Florida so I stayed at Mom's best friend's house – Ruthie Nadler. When I was better and wanting to do something nice for Ruthie for seeing me back to health, I called BY and asked him for five seats (Ruthie, her 3 children and me) for a Gilbert & Sullivan performance that was in town. Of course it was sold out, but BY told me where to go to pick up the tickets and they were in the second row!

I used that office on Milk Street as the business address for Gilman Garages, Inc. and ran my first ads weekends in the Boston Post, Herald and Globe newspapers. I advertised to deliver a pre-cut garage or to install a fully built one. I arranged for Grossman Lumber Company to deliver the materials on an unmarked flatbed truck. I sold five garages that summer. My wife and I were living in an apartment at 4 Kilsyth Terrace on the Brighton/Brookline border and I drafted Ricky the apartment unit handyman there to assist me in building one of the first garages I sold. It was in Marblehead, Massachusetts. It was

Leonard Gilman

fun and I enjoyed the challenge of figuring out how to hang the garage door.

Somehow I got through the winter, and the next year I sold 29 garages. I had hired my friend Marvin Gould to sell garages on a commission basis and he sold several.

REVERE BEACH PARKWAY

My father had invested in the Gil Wyner Construction Company (a road builder). Gil W was a great guy. He had the contract to re-route the Revere Beach Parkway in Everett, Mass. The state had taken many properties by eminent domain that were in the way of the new highway. One of the buildings was a steel warehouse of about 3,000 square feet. Gil said I could have the building if I wanted it. I sure did. It might have been 1956. I had now incorporated as Gilbilt Lumber Company and I occupied that small metal warehouse and a strip of land on the Revere Beach Parkway in Everett, Mass. I recall going to the Boston Public Library and reading up on how to build small wood frame buildings and learning the names of the various structural members. I was hesitatingly dipping a foot into the water. I had advertised for a carpenter and hired Bill Allen. Together we built a one room cabin atop which I had placed the sign "Gilbilt Garages". It was Gilbilt's first office.

Now Gilbilt was off and running, but only at a snail's pace. There was still considerable highway traffic past my highway construction site and Bill Allen and I built two garages; one on either side of my small office. That office had a wood floor which was laid directly over dirt. There was neither heat nor a bathroom. I hired Barbara Ferson to be my secretary/bookkeeper. Barbara was a local girl so she could go home when she had to use a rest room or for lunch. My only year round employee was Bill Allen a very skilled master carpenter. I remember that spring and later that winter how Barbara's feet and mine froze from the cold coming up through the floor in that unheated office (a small wood frame building about 10 x 10). We survived.

Gilbilt's first office. 1956 in Everett, MA, It had: electricity and, telephones, but no heat!

I had a dream that I could do in New England what I had seen Myles do in Minnesota. I was like the "Little Train that Could", but after a year I was under pressure to vacate my "free" property as the highway construction was accelerating and I knew I would have to relocate.

1956 was a fun year and many nights I would meet Marvin Gould, my childhood friend and only salesman, late at night in the parking lot of the apartment house where we both lived. We would be returning from sales calls and we would review sales pitches....what seemed to work, etc.

I guess that would have been the summer I hired my old shoe business mentor Larry Haiman. Larry was a good salesman. Misery must have been looking for company and I offered him a full partnership for $500. I guess prospects must have seemed dim for he turned down the offer. I never offered again.

1958–1962: ESTABLISHING GILBILT ON RT. 3A IN BURLINGTON, MA

I hustled and bought a vacant hilly piece of land near Rts. 3 and 128 in Burlington, Mass.

It might have been my third year in business – I invested all my profits and capital to date ($10,000) and in late fall of 1957 I bought a narrow seven acre hilly site in Burlington, Massachusetts on Route 3A, just north of Route 128. Marvin Gould was still working with me and in old home movies he can be seen riding on Don Parker's bulldozer that winter clearing the land. I had my pre-fab steel factory building dismantled and moved from Everett to Burlington. After Bill Allen, my first full-time employees were Don Parker and Pop and Bobby Westcott. Those three worked for me until I sold the company in 1969. I had now moved Gilbilt from the Revere Beach Parkway to Burlington, Mass. The location was perfect, but the topography was terrible.

I bought that first property for Gilbilt in the winter time since the ground was still partially frozen, and when the snow started to melt I saw ledge outcroppings which had to be removed. I hired a blasting company and the foreman to my amazement was handling and tossing around sticks of dynamite. To prove that was safe, he had me hold some sticks of dynamite until after just a few moments I started to get nauseous – a typical reaction when holding dynamite too long. As you may have noticed, I am still writing this history of Gilbilt, so I did not blow myself up that day while horsing around with sticks of dynamite.

The 10 acre site in Burlington had about 250' of frontage on Route 3A, and it was only an easy Jim Rice throw from the cloverleaf off of Route 128. I immediately erected four different styles of garages, one rather conventional summer cottage - the "Franklin", and a traffic stopping A frame vacation home, all in an arc around the circular entrance driveway. That Franklin cottage or "vacation home" as I termed it in newspaper ads had a front porch beneath the extended roof line that was the width of the building. After a few years there were Franklin cottages on the lakes of Winnipesaukee, Sebago, Long, Belgrade, Rangeley and other popular vacation areas throughout northern New England.

I had started to advertise on WBZ-TV on the Don Kent and Frank Chase weather and agricultural program the "Daily Almanac". It was a live show at 6:30AM for 15 minutes. Don and Frank visited a site in Woburn, Mass. and were filmed helping to erect one of my garages. The film was edited down to a commercial which also showed my wife Debbie driving into a garage with our poodle Val in the backseat. I had borrowed my father's Chevy convertible for that. My ad agency hired a group who created a singing jingle ("Gilbilt, Gilbilt...no money down, low payments, Gilbilt, Gilbilt, Gilbilt Garages"). The TV exposure was terrific particularly in Maine, New Hampshire and Vermont where farm folk tuned in to get morning produce prices at the Boston wholesale markets, and I was amazed at how many people watched it and knew of Gilbilt and its relationship with Don Kent the "Weatherman". Don had weather tipsters scattered all over the North Country (Maine, New Hampshire and Vermont). They would all be tele-typing him the weather where they were. He would collate it all and, then to finalize his forecast for the day, he would seemingly disregard all his volunteered input, open a window, look out and based on the clouds and wind he observed, make his "best guess" and create his report. I frequently sat in his office as he went live to New England farmers with his show. We had many laughs together. He helped Gilbilt grow.

I bought my first "new" truck in the summer of 1958. I had started to run several crews and needed a more reliable truck than the used one I started with which came from Goldie's Graveyard in Quincy, Mass. I sent that one back to Goldie and bought my first new truck; an International. I had a truck body builder stretch the chassis and install hoisting pistons beneath the truck bed so the driver could tilt up the truck bed and roll off a complete panelized garage or cottage.

I had ads in the papers every Sunday each with a coupon to be clipped. My salesman Larry and I eagerly awaited the mailman to see where we would be going to try to sell a garage. At times there were enough coupons that a regular route could be established and one of us would venture into Maine, New Hampshire or Vermont for 3-4 days of visiting prospective customers. I adopted the saying I featured in ads, badges and on postcards; "P.O.M.G.", which stood for "Peace of Mind Guaranteed". Everyone liked it including the attorney for a jeweler in Hartford who claimed it was his copyright. Sometimes it's easier to give way than make war, and I discontinued that campaign.

A CLUNKY ORANGE FORKLIFT WORKING
ON A HILL

The topography problem was that my property was the side of an extended hill which made every experience loading and unloading trucks a 'hold your breath' moment.

I had purchased a relic of a ten ton Ross forklift truck. It might have recently celebrated its 30th birthday and it really deserved to be given a proper and well-earned retirement. I had bought it from a used equipment company in Allston and had a mechanic add power steering which sort of and sometimes worked. The "power" steering was for the most part applied by the operator's arms and the machinery cooperated with hiccups and bursts of intermittent power. There was a Sunday morning when I had gone in to work. With no one around I was using the fork lift to restack lumber. That cantankerous forklift had fork extensions of close to 8' so it could pick up an entire panelized residential garage or cottage and load it onto a flatbed truck. I was stacking a pallet load of 2x6 dimension lumber and had the load elevated while I stepped out of the lift truck cab to slide a few 2x4 "sleepers" into place so I could then lower the load onto the sleepers and back the lift truck away. Suddenly the lift truck groaned as it often did, and the load slipped down a fraction of an inch. Yep, it dropped just enough that my hand was in its way and when I nervously removed my hand I saw that the pressure of the slipped load had been just enough to crack my wedding band. Later, I had the ring soldered properly, but I would often look at the soldered joint in wonderment feeling that that the strength of my wedding ring saved my hand.

Lenny's "Angel in the sky" was watching over him that day. I gave Debbie an extra kiss when I got home that Sunday afternoon.

Anyway, that old forklift chugged around always looking like it would fall over due to the slope of the land. It never did.

Another memory of my time in that unheated steel workshop in Burlington is of the winters, and how my carpenters kept an old empty oil drum blazing with scraps of cut off lumber. It was winter time and we weren't that busy. In retrospect I now wonder if perhaps they weren't "creating" lumber scraps to stay warm.

INNOVATING AND GROWING

When I decided to embark on my career as the 'garage king of New England' (tongue in cheek), I didn't have a background in construction. My father was a dress manufacturer. Actually, this was to become my basic competitive advantage – no prior conceived opinions about "but, it was always done this way." I was going down "the road not taken".

It might have been 1958 – my third year at advertising and building garages. Now I was advertising consistently in the Sunday Boston Globe. My rep there was Howard Flanagan and he was most helpful in assisting me with display layouts. I used an ad agency in Boston and from my darkroom at my childhood home in Newton, which had not yet been dismantled, I was able to "create" montages of huge forklifts moving stacks of lumber around my "virtual" lumberyard for my first sales brochure. I was learning fast and devouring trade magazines about innovative developments in residential construction.

I had read an article about roof trusses which were stronger than the conventional framing techniques passed down from the days of the Pilgrims. Trusses were being hyped as not only being stronger but for relatively small homes and other incidental wood frame structures they were constructed from 2x4's as opposed to 2x6's. I read about a man who had developed hardware called the "H-Brace". It was a connector clip which held together and fastened the chord components of trusses. He was in Miami. I told Debbie, "We're going to Miami, part vacation, and part learning." My accountant told me I could write a "working" trip off as a deductible expense (providing only that my garage biz was showing a profit, and it barely was).

In Miami I spent two days with the "H-Brace" inventor who also grew orchids in his greenhouse. Debbie was delighted with all the orchids Harold gave her, and I was boning up on engineering data about roof trusses.

Back home in Burlington, Mass. I had a display park of garages and cottages. I had become Harold's first "H-Brace" dealer in New England. Perhaps Harold thought I was going to build thousands of vacation homes. What I did was force my new found education about lightweight roof trusses on skeptical building inspectors. I had Gilbilt's carpenters build and put on display a section of a roof built with trusses. I loaded up the top of that small roof section with concrete blocks. Once again I was going down 'a road not taken'. Eventually after a few rejections, the combination of the engineering data, and that striking visual display, I was able to convince more and more inspectors to allow 2x4 roof trusses!

Another "first" I was involved with about then were stapling hammers and then power nailing of roof shingles. Wow! For a century or more roof shingles had been nailed with ¾" roofing nails – a slow and tedious job which led to many a sore and blackened finger-nail. I had been approached by a Bostitch salesman to try out a stapling hammer and I quickly saw the time savings involved. The stapler held a cartridge of about 400 staples, and was swung similar to a hammer. One of my 'old-time' carpenters, Pop Westcott, resisted this new way but when he saw young Jimmy Lawlor fastening roof shingles almost twice as fast he gave in and accepted this revolutionary technique. I soon realized why I had been given six of these hammers as freebies. My carpenters were the guinea pigs for field testing this new tool. The problem was that the Bostitch staple hammer jammed too frequently. I became expert at clearing the jammed hammers each night at home. In discussions with Bostitch they eventually shelved the stapling hammers and developed the nail guns in use today. Soon thereafter I bought pneumatic auto-nailer guns and once again had to convince building inspectors that although not yet recognized in printed building codes that they did just as good a job and eventually they became accepted everywhere.

My first advertising agency was a small shop in Waltham, Mass. I would visit the owner at his office in the basement of his home, but after two office visits I changed agencies. His basement walls were covered with charcoal sketches of the progression of his wife's pregnancy (she was nude). Too disconcerting especially when she came in to serve us coffee while walking tilted backwards. My next agency was Ray Barron and Ray did a great job for me. Many years later my daughter Susan worked for him.

TAKING THE BAD WITH THE GOOD

July 3, 1958. Some dates just stay with you. This particular date I can readily recall because the confluence of events were sufficient to bring tears of exhaustion and frustration. One of my salesmen had sold a two car garage to a farm family in Maynard, Mass. The concrete slab was scheduled to be poured on the morning of July 3. The masons scheduled were Joe Silva (my #1 mason) and his helper Bob O'Melia. Early that morning Joe's wife called to tell me he was in the hospital (some minor issue that caused him to miss only a few days of work). I made some quick calls but was unable to replace him. Bob O'Melia was a big, strong, husky youngster who had worked slabs before with Joe. He said he and I could do the job, plus it was already too late cancel the Red-Mix scheduled for delivery at 9:00AM.

On the previous day Joe and Bob had completed the slab prep work for what is called a monolithic pour - a total concrete slab poured all at one time directly on the ground with deeper and wider edges for footings.

It was an overcast day and the Redi-Mix truck was right on time. Bob was a hustler and the two of us were soon sweating as we screed and floated the surface of wet concrete. We took a break letting the slab set up while we had our lunch. Then Bob took over and with a large, smooth steel trowel he polished off the surface. By then it must have been the middle of the afternoon and as we were getting ready to pack up our tools and leave, the rains came. First a drizzle, then slashing rain. There was nothing to do but add to the moisture with tears, as the surface of the slab was ruined. Bob said he was due at home soon, and there was nothing we could do anyway.

I assured the lady of the house that the surface would be repaired to be as good as new after the holiday, and it was, but written sixty years later I can still remember the effort, the expense, the frustration and the tears.

Bob O'Melia was an A#1 type employee – hardworking, honest and loyal. Why do the good guys die young? Bob passed away suddenly from a blood disorder. I don't think he made it to age 35.

It was about that time that Sam Cresta and eventually several of his younger brothers, or perhaps cousins, came to work at Gilbilt. The Cresta men posed a historical coincidence that is difficult for me to understand or explain. I'll try. In the 1930's and 1940's my father, Herman Gilman, was a dress manufacturer (Boston Maid) with a factory in Waltham, Mass. In its maximum employment years Dad employed perhaps a similar number as Gilbilt/Continental did at its peak. As a child, I got to know the three Iodice brothers who were employed in my father's factory. They befriended me and I them. Now in the early 1960's and onward, I employed Cresta's: Sam, Armando, Mario, Nick and perhaps another. History was repeating for father and son, each with valued employees from an expanded Italian/American family all of whom were dependable, loyal and gifted.

Sam Cresta was all that, plus he was a natural leader. Easily one of my best business decisions was the Saturday I drove to his home to convince him to stay at Gilbilt and be my company foreman. At the time I employed perhaps 25 men and Sam had worked for me for only two years. I talked to Sam and his wife Virginia that day telling them of how far I thought Sam and I could take Gilbilt. We shook hands that day and that handshake created an unbroken bond of friendship that lasted beyond the time I retired to Florida. When Sam eventually retired from Continental, men and women involved in the then greatly expanded home manufacturing industry throughout northeastern U.S. honored him at a testimonial banquet. He had helped to father that industry. I was so proud of and for him.

Decades later I would fly from Florida to Sam's home in New Hampshire to say goodbye to my friend. Sadly, I was a day too late.

A NAME CHANGE & BUILDING THE TEAM

The next two years found Gilbilt Garages had become Gilbilt Lumber Corp. It was now not uncommon for us to ship 3-4 buildings a day. I had added to our fleet with two White long bodied cab-overs.

Look Dad! There goes another Gilbilt garage. 1958.

Now Gilbilt had competition. A company called Atlantic Garages near New Bedford, Grossman Lumber Company, and a vacation home company on Cape Cod had become advertising competitors. Although not exactly a tourist attraction, Gilbilt's display park in Burlington became a rather busy place on weekends and I now had several more salesmen; Warren Greenough, Cy King (who died suddenly while working for me), Carl Selmer and Arthur Feldman rounded out the sales staff. My friend and neighbor Larry Haiman became the full-time Sales Manager. No longer wearing a sales cap I devoted myself to: planning advertising, materials purchasing, and scheduling the erection crews which necessitated me being the first in to work at 6:30AM. Gilbilt was being noticed and I had started buying lumber by the railcar load from Dick "Eggs" O'Brien who became a lifelong friend. Dick married my secretary Harriet and after Dick and I had each retired, my wife and I visited and stayed with the Obrien's in the Tampa area.

About that time I realized the difficulty of being the only company advertising garages so I created a phantom company. Now I had a "competitor" which helped build more public awareness about the need for a garage. I named that company "Ace Pre-Cut Garages". Ace ads had an order form directed to a P.O. Box and I recall my surprise when I went to the post office after Ace's first ads and discovered Ace actually had several orders! I have to assume Ace's ads, appearing on the same page as Gilbilt's ads, were actually helping Gilbilt since Gilbilt's Display Park was getting more and more traffic. Apparently people became sub-consciously more interested and aware of the need for a garage when they saw two companies advertising for their business. Almost all of our ads were placed in the sports sections of the weekend papers.

Gilbilt's "A" Frame vacation home was popular in the mountain resort communities of Maine and Vermont.

The summer of 1958 was a break-through time for Gilbilt. I now had a full Display Park in Burlington which included two vacation cottages and three garages. The Franklin cottage was the most popular we sold. But the A Frame vacation home pulled in a lot of traffic. We did sell A Frames in the ski resort areas of Dover, Vermont, the Rangeley Lakes and as far north as Moosehead Lake. Moosehead Lake is the largest lake in the state of Maine. I was blessed with a wonderful team of carpenters led by crew chiefs: Sam Cresta, Frankie Morin, the Westcott's, Ray Beaudoin, and Ray Samson. With a crew they would drive one of the big flatbed trucks, and a pickup with tools and a generator, and their sleeping bags, far north into the hinterlands of New England where they would erect enough of a vacation home to

27

sleep in the first night and complete it on the second day. Believe me, in the late 1950's some of those now densely populated resort areas were desolate. In particular I remember a cottage we installed at Moosehead Lake (about 250 miles north of Burlington, Massachusetts). It was for a retired Navy admiral whose habit was to fire his rifle each morning to get a replying shot from a person across the lake to assure each other they were ok.

Archie Bunker wasn't the only one to say, "Those were the days." Can you imagine a crew of carpenters doing that today?

HO-HO-HO AND BAH HUMBUG!
A CHRISTMAS TALE

The winter of 1958/59 promised to be a bleak one for my then little company. In the summer and fall of '58 I had employed perhaps 35 men (all either carpenters or all around laborers, and a few masons). Of that number there were 8 to 10 I could ill afford to lay off over the winter months. In addition to being my most skilled employees, they were my good friends. I had met most of their wives and children. I had taken a lesson from my father's 'playbook' and each summer I had hired a bus to take my employees families to Canobie Lake Park in Salem, NH for amusement rides, a lunch, and just being together in a non-business situation where we were all just friends. I enjoyed those outings as much as the kids. To lay those men off for the winter would decimate the company since I knew there would be little chance of re-employing them the following spring. The conundrum I faced was what to do with the highest paid men on my payroll during the coming winter months. At that time my company was only three or four years young. We sold residential garages and vacation homes throughout Massachusetts and northern New England. That involved pouring the concrete slab and erecting the structure which we pre-fabbed in our un-heated steel building in Burlington, Mass. The property I owned and occupied eventually became the access road into the Burlington Mall. Unfortunately the man I eventually sold it to was a "blind' for the mall developer so I did not get paid the true value of the property.

The solution to my winter payroll problem was suggested by Don McCue. Don was not one of my skilled carpenters but he was young, agile and an eager worker (exactly how "eager", I would only later find out). Don came to me and said he hoped I would employ him through that winter, and he offered a financial solution. His uncle was one of the major Christmas tree sellers with the prime location he had annually in Haymarket Square in downtown Boston. Don had worked for his uncle for several Christmas tree seasons and he claimed to know the ins and outs of that all cash business. My interest was piqued.

Through 'connections' I secured exclusive sales locations at: Zayres (now TJ Maxx) parking lots in Medford and Natick, and at JM Fields parking lots in Everett and Lynn. Don told me about a Christmas tree wholesaler in Thetford Mines, Quebec, Canada. After a few conversations with that man – it required a translator since he spoke only French – it was agreed we would meet to sign an agreement.

It was a bitter cold day spitting sleet when, with my sales manager Larry, we arrived at a bar in Thetford Mines, Quebec. We had driven through the night and now here we were at 6:00 in the morning shivering in a bar on an early October morning. Back home it was Indian summer. Here I felt I was in a foreign country. I was.

The owner of the tree farm was waiting for us with his interpreter. We negotiated back and forth. I felt we were signing an Armistice. After we eventually reached a deal, the seller insisted and we all toasted each other with shots of quantro! I had signed an agreement to purchase 20,000 Christmas trees – 5,000 for each location. Truckload deliveries were to commence on Columbus Day!

I BOUGHT 'EM, NOW I MUST SELL 'EM

Think about it. Thousands of evergreen trees to be kept from dropping their needles for seven weeks. Difficult? Yes. Impossible? No. I had this growing mound of bundled trees in my small lumber yard in Burlington, Massachusetts being sprinkled 3 times a week then re-covered with reflective insulation to deflect the sun and warm temperatures. Silliness? You bet. Did it work? Sort of.

The sale of Christmas trees, being an all cash business, unfortunately attracts the criminal element. Don told me many stories about theft and robbery. He also told me that most tree vendors carry a gun. I had never been a cowboy and the last thing I wanted was for my employees to be gun carrying representatives. I had my carpenters build 4 small guardhouses and deliver them to the sales sites. They were to serve two purposes: to provide a place my "salesmen" could go to get out of the weather and stay warm, and a place an all-night guard could stay to "protect" inventory. We never discussed how that was to be accomplished. Perhaps my carpenters armed themselves with staple guns? Each guardhouse was about four foot square and contained a stool and a kerosene fueled salamander. The one window would have to provide a venting for the fumes.

We opened our four tree stands two days before Thanksgiving. Then "Mr. Winter" paid Eastern Massachusetts a visit. He stayed for three weeks. We froze our tuchas' off! No matter how we dressed we (my carpentry "sales crew", my sales manager and I) were all numb. We truly felt we were in a frozen forest waiting for the Battle of the Bulge. My father and an uncle made the rounds of our four sites picking up cash, and my sales crew had to be rotated in shifts due to the frigid blasts and drifting snow sweeping through those parking lots. The kerosene salamanders provided some respite from the cold, but the fumes sent each of us home streaked with black greasy soot and looking like coal miners from the early 1900's. Each night once I got home, I would undress inside the front door so as to not 'contaminate' my house and head to a hot bathtub where my wife would bring me a thermos of coffee and bowls of steaming soup. Stacks of one dollar bills had to be counted and banded. Ever counted a few thousand dollars in crumpled dollar bills? Your hands, like mine, would become cracked and cut… so much so that you would sleep with Vaseline coated hands in cotton gloves.

Selling a Christmas tree can be a novel experience. Everyone wants a "short, fat, bushy one". In those days most everyone lived in a home with ceilings that were 8' or less. Despite that, most men would buy a 9' or a 10' tree. Size can be deceptive standing in an open parking lot while your scrotum is shriveling. The trees had to be continually spritzed and then severely shaken to prevent freezing. Now, how to sell a tree: You stand behind it while holding it up for a customer. Then when the customer asks to see the other side you merely do a 360 degree turnaround without loosening your grasp on the tree. Understand? Same side, and of course the best side is always shown. That worked more times than not, but even when it didn't both the buyer and seller always had a good laugh. One last thing; those who celebrate Christmas all want a tree but the actual decision time at purchase comes close to that of seeing the dentist or buying a car without your spouse's approval. Indecision rules! And many Christmas tree buyers seem to not enjoy buying their tree!

Okay, now it is around December 20. Almost all the good trees have been sold. We all feel like the Abominable Snowman. Money has been banked and I can keep my good carpentry crew chiefs through the remainder of the winter. What to do with the thousand or so trees remaining? Wholesale them. I made a contact with a New Jersey State

Trooper who had a tree lot at the Fulton Fish Market in NYC. I cut a deal with him and rent a tractor-trailer which we load and send to him with one of my foremen riding shotgun. Six hours later, almost as expected the trooper calls to tell me "These trees are junk". He offers me ½ the agreed price. Me stubborn? You betcha. I tell my foreman to take the whole load and leave them free at a Salvation Army site.

Almost at the end of this saga.

DISENTANGLING MYSELF FROM DICTATORS

December 23, 1958. and I succumb to this battle. I am sick in bed. The bed is covered with stacks and stacks of banded dollar bills. My wife Debbie takes care of the banking and I decide we have earned a vacation. We book a flight to the Dominican Republic and on the 29th we fly there. Bear in mind that beautiful island country was still ruled by the dictator Rafael Trujillo. Our hotel is picture perfect, but empty of guests. The only sounds in the Casino are of the dealers shuffling stacks of chips, or of a roulette ball being endlessly whirled around.

It is now the morning of New Year's Day, 1959 I awake to foreboding silence. Our window is open but even the birds seem to have disappeared. Looking out the window I see soldiers setting up a machine gun on a tripod. I throw on some clothes and quick-step to a concierge in the lobby. "Sir, have you not heard? Fulgencio Batista has been overthrown in Cuba by Fidel Castro and Batista is expected here at our hotel momentarily." I dash upstairs and tell Debbie, "We gotta get outa here!" Batista and Trujillo aren't enough, but Argentinean Colonel Juan Peron is in exile down the street. Enough already! We pack and cab to the airport to take the first flight to anywhere leaving soonest. And that is how I came to discover the island paradise country of Haiti, then ruled by Papa Doc Duvalier. My first experience in Haiti takes place as we are leaving the airport on the way to our hotel. I am shooting movies out the cab window when the cabbie pulls over to an armed soldier. The grim soldier tells me I am not allowed to take pictures of any poverty. What else is there here to photograph? After considerable discussion I am allowed to retrieve my camera from him for bail of $5.00.

Postscript: My trusted employee Don was arrested the following year on the steps of a bank he had just robbed at gunpoint. I wonder if, and how much, he might have stolen from me as a "silent" Christmas tree partner? Can you believe my life? All wonderful memories!

I was invited to appear on Boston radio/TV station WEEI regarding Gilbilt's accomplishments, and plans for the future. While waiting in a small dressing room for my turn to be interviewed I chatted with another guest, a tall good looking man named Robert Goulet. He had a big, booming baritone voice. I saw him again just three years later on Broadway where he was starring in "Camelot". I guess that radio show appearance brought us each good luck. When he sang "If Ever I Would Leave You", the lyrics and the power he put into it, still give me goosebumps. Over the years since, whenever I hear him sing that song I immediately, automatically think back to our meeting in the small make-up room, nervously chatting about our dreams.

Gilbilt stayed in Burlington for about five years during which time, without realizing it, I was building the team which would enable the company to grow as rapidly as it did. Soon I needed a larger (and more level) property. I looked thirty miles north and found the ideal location for my company in Nashua, NH. It was an abandoned air strip paralleling the mainline of the B&M railroad and the Merrimack River. It had frontage on Route 3A which I needed to build what would become Gilbilt Display Park – 4 garages, a Franklin cottage, and a complete 3 BR split-level home. I was "good to go."

MOVING TIME AGAIN

Once again it was time to move. I was aware of the tax advantages of operating a business in New Hampshire and living there so I made an initial foray to Nashua, NH. My first contact was with Sam Tamposi ("Mr. New Hampshire Realtor"). Sam showed me some properties West of Nashua heading towards Milford and almost as an after-thought an abandoned twenty acre WWII emergency airstrip on the South side of Nashua. The site lay alongside the Merrimack River. Sam introduced me to Nashua Mayor Mario Vagge and I drove home wondering if I was thinking on too grandiose a scale. I liked the airstrip site for several reasons; it was dead flat and it had the Boston & Maine RR paralleling it. I don't remember the name of the land owner other than he was a Frenchman and he lived in a white house which was to become my office for several years.

When Sam first pointed out the property as we drove past I told him I was familiar with it. About two years prior my college friend and next door neighbor in Framingham, Massachusetts, Ezzie Sheffres and his family, and my family were returning from a Memorial Day vacation in northern New Hampshire. Was my choice of a resort named Christmas Tree Inn prophetic, or just ironic? Perhaps you remember feeding the bears at Clark's Trading Post on the highway north of Concord, NH? Well, the Sunday holiday traffic going home was bumper to bumper so as we passed through Nashua we pulled into a restaurant by the name of the White Swan for a quick bite. After placing our orders we realized that other customers were just sitting around and no one in the restaurant was being served. I went into the kitchen (ala my father's style) and saw the cooks were also just sitting around. Someone said something about not working anymore until they were paid. We left. Two years later I found myself buying that then abandoned restaurant which occupied the highway frontage of the airport site which Gilbilt would own until I sold the company. Long after moving to Florida we still had various cocktail glasses and wine goblets from the White Swan restaurant.

Now, 60 years later, I can easily understand why Debbie said, "No way are we moving to Nashua." She had lived her early years through high school in the small, pastoral country town of Greenfield, Massachusetts, and then, after enjoying all the cultural benefits of living in the suburbs of a big city like Boston, she was reluctant to return to a small city. It all worked out.

1962 - Len Gilman purchases abandoned Nashua, NH airport property for Gilbilt Homes manufacturing facility. Seated: l-r: Len Gilman, Seller's attorney-Sam Bornstein, l-r: Nashua Mayor Mario Vagge, Attorney Warren Rudman (ten years from being elected U.S. Senator), Sam Tamposi, Aaron Harkaway (attorney for the seller), Larry Haiman - Gilbilt Sales Manager.

When I decided to relocate my then small company from Burlington, Massachusetts to Nashua, New Hampshire I was guided by two men who would become wonderful friends; Sam Tamposi and Warren Rudman. Sam was the Realtor who sold me the land onto which I moved my company. He later became a part owner of the Boston Red Sox. Warren was a few years younger than me. He had just established his law practice and I became his first client as he represented me when I bought the long since abandoned air-strip which was to be Gilbilt's home. Warren would go on to be Attorney General of NH, and then a prominent United States Senator. *Was it my influence on others which propelled them, or was it the influence of others which motivated me? Either way, Nashua was lucky for all three of us!*

A year after I re-settled Gilbilt to Nashua, I convinced Debbie it was time to move our family there. It would have been about 1962 when I moved my family from Framingham, Massachusetts to Nashua, New Hampshire. I could not imagine that only ten years later we would be moving to Florida. Sam Tamposi introduced me to a local builder and we bought a home on Alice Drive. It was a comfortable two story with a picket fenced backyard. We became active in the Temple and I into Kiwanis, and we were welcomed into the community. One of our good friends was Mayor Mario Vagge who lived a few streets away. Our three girls would visit Mario on Halloween and always came home with home baked Italian pastry.

My good friend Sam Tamposi bought panelized houses from me to salt some of his vacant residential properties, and I bought a vacant 5 acre lot from him. On an opposite corner of the street Warren Rudman bought a house lot. I built each of our homes there on Indian Rock Road. Then my good friend and next door neighbor from Framingham, and college fraternity brother, Ezzie Sheffres completed the cycle by surprising us when he became our neighbor again.

Gilbilt's sign on the Daniel Webster Highway in Nashua, NH – 1963.

Warren's father owned Old Colony Furniture, a manufacturer of the highest quality wood furniture. I still have the beautiful dining room table I bought from Ed Rudman, and I am proud to know that one exactly like mine is, or was, in the White House. Ed would come daily to observe the progress of Warren's house. I remember how he questioned my foreman on the use of staples on both the plywood sub-flooring and the roof shingles.

1962–1969: GROWING UP IN NASHUA

Shortly after opening Gilbilt's first factory in Nashua I realized it was time to divest myself of one of the many hats I was wearing. I hit a home run when I hired Paul Kidder to handle the sensitive and critical scheduling of the installation crews. Each installation crew was headed by a crew chief who as the lead carpenter was responsible to finish the job while keeping the entire crew and the owner/buyer cheerful. In those days we had two sets of brothers which at times made juggling the make-up of each crew a challenging exercise in balancing its personalities with its capabilities. It required a fine touch similar to that of a symphony conductor and, always with a laugh Paul satisfied everyone. Like me, when I started the company, Paul came aboard with no knowledge of wood frame construction, but he was a mother hen to everyone and their contrasting abilities and egos. Paul was big – an easy 300 pounder who was also athletically quick enough to start and be on Gilbilt's first softball team. He was a major part of both the softball team and the corporate team until the time I sold the company. Years later I was consultant to a start-up modular homes company in Florida and I recruited Paul to come to Florida to be the general manager of that company. He and his wife Peggy were our good friends and my wife and I welcomed the Kidders as they married off their daughter Kathleen in our home on Singer Island, Florida.

I had the "lucky" metal building I started with on the Revere Beach Parkway in Everett, moved to Rt. 3A in Burlington, and finally to Nashua, NH. Eventually I had that building torn down and replaced it with a metal structure of about 8000 SF. Then, in 1969, I had erected the 69,000 SF building which became the first factory in the USA expressly designed and constructed specifically for the manufacture of modular homes.

A typical Gilbilt garage & cottage ad – 1963.

As a kid growing up in the home of a garment manufacturer I came to understand what "a new season" meant. For me it meant sprucing up Gilbilt's Display Park. All the buildings on display were given a fresh coat of paint. Usually throughout March I would be placing increasingly larger garage and cottage ads in various Sunday papers until perhaps the first Sunday in April the ads would declare a "Grand Opening" day at Gilbilt. On display ringing the parking lot, there would be a half dozen garages, one or two cottages and a split level home. It was made to be a festive occasion with balloons, patriotic bunting and usually an onsite disc jockey from a local radio station. He played music over loudspeakers and interviewed people asking them where they had come from that day. We tried to create a carnival spirit with the rebirth of spring and invariably our parking lot was filled every Opening Day.

At one of Gilbilt's "Grand Opening" Sundays the weather was overcast all afternoon. Our usual traffic had all but dwindled to nothing by 5:00PM. I was sitting in a room in the front of the sales office just shooting the breeze with a few of my salesmen. Our attention was drawn to a car coming off the highway and circling down past the lineup of garages. We all watched as it finally stopped in front of the Franklin cottage. A steady cold drizzle had started. Rafael Mendez, the famous Latin America trumpet player was still being broadcast on the outdoor speakers as we watched an older gent and his lady park and walk onto the covered Franklin porch. In the sales office not a peep. It had been a long day and I could sense that not one of the salesmen (they worked on a draw against commission) had little interest to go out in the rain, perhaps for a "tire kicker"? I did. I had no raincoat but I figured I would be standing under the covered porch of the cottage. The prospects were a delightful couple. They had just bought a lakefront lot on either Little Squam or Squam Lake in the New Hampshire Lakes region. He was the President of Boston University. He called me the following day and said he would be back the following weekend. Yes he did, and he bought an enlarged version of the Franklin cottage. Perseverance.

Opening Day at Gilbilt Display Park. Debbie and Len Gilman, Nashua radio personality. 1962.

By 1962 the transition from garages to panelized homes was almost complete. In just the few years I had been in Nashua I had made a good friend in Dan Murdock. Dan was the de facto operating CEO of the Second National Bank in Nashua. We often met for lunch at the Green Ridge Turkey Farm Restaurant to be joined by Vic the restaurant's owner. I had become a major bank customer and occasionally borrowed money from the bank with only a phone call for short term business loans. It was in this period that more and more media were writing about the many different forms of "pre-fab" homes and the advantages of them. Through Dan I was invited to speak at a New Hampshire Bankers Association luncheon in Concord, New Hampshire. I spoke about manufactured homes perhaps for twenty minutes and then answered questions for another half hour. In the weeks that followed I received several notes from bankers who had attended that luncheon thanking me for enlightening them on the advantages to a builder and a home buyer of a manufactured home. That luncheon meeting soon proved to be a boon to my business. Suddenly banks were willing to grant approval to mortgage applications for a Gilbilt home! Prior to my meeting many of the bankers were skeptical about the quality of construction of a "pre-fab". Amazing, after that one luncheon meeting I was able to use the names of those who sent me complimentary notes as a reference to doubting bank loan officers.

My foreman, Sam Cresta, and I traveled to Pittsburgh where we watched a demo of a steel framing table. I had the prototype assembly table shipped to Nashua. Don Parker and I flew to Fort Wayne, Indiana and watched a demo of a truck mounted crane. I ordered that equipment and had it mounted on the rear of my first tractor-trailer. It was my first Mack truck and I saved the souvenir Mack ashtray as a remembrance of that order. I was home sick on the day the Mack was delivered. Don drove it to my home so I could see our truck/crane. I was so proud. Now it is not unusual to see a similar truck mounted crane every day.

Sam and I doodled on paper to create the various grab devices that Paul Caron, a local machinist, welded so the long and bulky house fabricated panels could be hoisted safely into position. Even today I have not seen roof truss carrying devices as efficient as we used in the early 1960's. At the Home Builder's Show at McCormick Place in

Chicago I bought a press through which roof trusses would be rolled to stamp in the steel chord connector plates. The name of the game was "innovation". Do it better. Do it faster. Do it safer.

I haunted trade shows in Boston, Chicago, Houston, etc., and although I enjoyed adding new machinery, such as overhead cranes and other equipment, which always intrigued me and benefitted my small company greatly, I always knew that my greatest assets were the people I employed.

Len at work – circa 1964 (before cordless phones).

In those years, and for many after, a garage and even a vacation home could be financed by an FHA Home Improvement Loan. In Minneapolis Myles Fiterman had shown me how to complete and submit that paperwork and I placed all that paper through the First National Bank of Boston. The bank's rep would call on me monthly in Nashua and we always ended up at a several hour luncheon at the

Green Ridge Turkey Farm. He was quite the raconteur and he liked drinking that yucky green creme de menthe liqueur straight and it seemed to be a contest as to who would call it quits first. We became good friends, and I know that partially because of my friendship with him, and of course because of the volume of business we were writing on the bank's FHA financing plan, that many shaky deals were accepted by the bank. Despite that, they told me that the payment records of Gilbilt Homes' buildings borrowers were close to 100%. I do remember that on at least two occasions, somewhere in the 'boondocks' of New Hampshire, we actually sold a garage which would be used as a home. Yes, it was financed by FHA. It was a "real" home improvement.

The upside-down garage was a traffic-stopper on Rt. 3A in Nashua, NH – 1965.

Gilbilt Village Display Park – Circa 1963.

PERINI TO THE RESCUE!

There were a few bumps in the road though. Once I came within a day of having to lay off my entire crew of carpenters due to a lack of orders. It might have been not quite spring of 1963. With a few sporadic orders I had been able to keep my shop carpenters and most all of the outside erection crew chiefs on the payroll that winter. This time the roadbuilder Perini Corp came to my rescue.

Massachusetts was expanding its network of highways encircling Boston. The inner ring was Rt. 128 and the outer ring was Rt. 495. The state bid requirement for these multi –million dollar highway construction jobs always included a small building for engineers and draftsmen, and a sanitary building with urinals, a shower and hand sinks. Both buildings had to be safely portable (capable of withstanding the shock [cracked interiors] of being hoisted by a crane onto a truck to be re-located).

A few months previously some State of Massachusetts engineer had heard of my company, and in the mail I received a request to design those two buildings. The Engineer's Office building was to include a draftsman's table and high chair, extra interior lighting, a closet and two metal desks and chairs. The Sanitary Building was to be as described above. Both buildings were to be 10' wide by 18' long (highway transportable on a lo-boy heavy duty trailer). One of my carpenters was a good draftsman and in two days I submitted a blueprint and specs for each building. They were designed to be built on a base of two 22' long 10"x10" Douglas fir skids with an iron strap at each end to enable the building to be hoisted into the air and/or dragged to a location.

Amazing! When I needed it most I got a call from the Perini Corporation – "Had I seen the bid request (for some particular highway construction job) calling for 8 each of the Engineers and Sanitary buildings in the Dodge Reports" (a bi-monthly bulletin mailed to all appropriate potential contractors for state of Mass. projects? When I told the man calling me I had not, he read off the bidding requirement," .... To include 16 portable buildings as designed by Gilbilt of Nashua, NH." Vundebar! Thanks to Perini that order enabled me to keep a base crew of ten key men employed for another month until spring orders started to come in.

It was with considerable pride, and a sigh of "thank-you Lou Perini", as I stood with my crew in Gilbilt's yard and watched Perini tractor trailer lo-boys haul away those shanties.

It was in 1963 or 1964 that I sponsored the first meeting (a dinner get together) of Gilbilt builder/dealers and what little competition I had. At this meeting I proposed the start of what eventually became the National Association of Building Manufacturers. The pre-fabricated home industry needed credibility and the formation of NABM seemed to be the antidote to any lingering dubious thoughts reminiscent of pre-fab Quonset huts, which many veterans from WWII might remember, and not with accompanying pleasant memories. I recruited Bob Wellman who was the sales manager for Hogdson Homes and Dan Donahue who had just started New England Homes to join with me in founding what would become NABM. I had help from Warren Pease who was a feature writer with the Nashua Telegraph and a contributing editor to the nationally distributed magazine titled "Building Supply News", both of which publications were enamored about the future of pre-fabricated homes.

Don Parker, my long-time employee and now manager of the company's fleet of trucks and drivers, found a source for adding several more used trailers to our growing fleet of vehicles and he had Joe Zarilla, an outside mason we had a close working relationship with, build a concrete block service garage with two large bays in which we could do necessary minor truck repairs and maintenance. We had by then installed a 1000 gallon fuel tank and were becoming more and more self-sufficient. Unfortunately, not all of Don's truck drivers were too cautious. One time when my father and accountant were visiting, Don knocked on my office door asking if I could step out of my meeting for a minute. He then explained that one of our tractor-trailer drivers had backed into my father's convertible making it even lower to the ground. I arranged for someone to drive them home and later that year while my parents were away on vacation I ordered and surprised them with a Jaguar.

In Nashua, success was on-going and within five years I had enlarged my factory several times and now had builder/dealers throughout New Hampshire, Maine and Vermont who were ordering and erecting Gilbilt pre-fabricated garages, cottages and homes.

State Champs – 1967.

The Long and Short of It

Gilbilt Homes first baseman Ed Kazakavich towers over third baseman Ray McEvoy providing Gilbilt with an unusual infield combination. Kazakavich, a newcomer to the Nashua scene stands in at 6-5. Both men have played key roles in Gilbilt's surge to the top in the Nashua Slo-Pitch Softball League. (Telegraphoto—Andruskevich)

The long and the short of it! Gilbilt's sponsored softball team was a winner!

A BIRD IN THE HAND?

Thanksgiving Day, 1964. I had gone to my office early that morning to take care of some paperwork while the building was quiet. Sometime around 9:00AM I am in my office and the door is closed. Suddenly I hear the breaking of a window and fear someone has broken into the building. Directly outside my office is my secretary's office and I can hear the noises of someone or something moving around. I go to the furthest corner of my office and dial the Nashua Police. I whisper into the phone, "Hi, this is Len Gilman at Gilbilt. Someone has just broken into my office building. I am in my office."

"Stay there. Do NOT confront him. A car is on the way."

Five minutes later I see two cops run past my window with guns drawn. A moment later I hear one of them calling out from my secretary's office, "Mr. G, you can come out now. We've captured the culprit." Yes, they had. A bird had flown through the window while apparently seeing through to the large window on the opposing corner wall. What I heard was the poor navigator thrashing out its life directly outside my office door. I went home. I had had enough excitement for one day.

The Associated Press picked up the story from the Nashua Telegraph and two days later my out of town in-laws were reading about the "burglar" at Gilbilt Homes in Nashua!

New England winters always posed a problem. Builders weren't disciplined to get foundations in the ground before the freeze. They had grown up thinking their only solution to winter was to make like a bear and hibernate. One winter I took a carload of my key people (Sam Cresta (company carpentry foreman), Larry Haiman (sales manager), Bob Westcott (lead crew chief), and Don Parker (traffic manager) on a motor trip to tour factories in Pennsylvania, Ohio and New Jersey. Not only were other owners hospitable but invariably I was able to recruit them to join the NABM. Sam Cresta was a sponge at absorbing new techniques we observed and then improving on them. I think it would be fair to say that Sam was easily the brightest craftsman and innovator in the development of the factory-built housing industry throughout its formative years.

Additional savings were achieved when the B&M RR added a spur track onto my property. Now we received our plywood and dimension lumber directly into our yard.

Highway signs scattered throughout Maine, New Hampshire, and Vermont.

I was using an ad agency in Manchester, New Hampshire and several highways north of us had billboards that proclaimed "Gilbilt Village ahead". I wish I had photos of the Batman and Robin series of Gilbilt billboards ("Holy Garage (or cottage), Robin, it's a Gilbilt").

SAN JUAN STIMULATED THOUGHTS
OF SELLING OUT

I was becoming concerned that as Gilbilt continued to grow, it seemed that the real beneficiary was the Mack truck dealer in Boston since more and more of my gains had to be re-invested in rolling equipment.

I remember the moment the first stirrings of thoughts to sell out were born. It was on a winter vacation with the family in San Juan, Puerto Rico in early 1969. We were in a large hotel nightclub watching Harry Belafonte ("Day-o, day-o") when I first started to ponder that selling Gilbilt made sense in many ways. Years later I wished I had given more thought to what I would do after I sold out.

The year 1969 was the decisive year for Gilbilt. I had decided to sell Gilbilt if a good buyer could be found. "Good" meaning more than just a good financial deal for my family. I also would only accept a situation which would enable me to keep my entire "family" of carpenters, drivers, draftsmen, office staff, etc. employed year round. They were my "Team". In those days, as you must appreciate, there were few factory-built panelized home manufacturers, and of the few in New England Gilbilt was the largest and most well-known. The many years of newspaper and TV advertising had created an even larger image of the company than we were in the minds of bankers, builders and the general public.

It was at that time I had also decided to enter into the manufacture of modular homes. I was torn; I was of a mind to sell my company, yet at the same time I was getting ready to expand it. This would necessitate a new and a larger factory, and Gilbilt, nurtured with so much love, was subtly seeking a new owner. I pushed the envelope and Gilbilt became the first company in the USA to operate out of a factory specifically designed for the manufacture of modular homes - "mods". I hired the design firm of Slayter Associates (somewhere in the Midwest) which company had experience in the design of the assembly and production lines of several mobile home factories, the most famous of which was Champion Mobile Homes. We broke ground in early1969.

In the meantime, I had accepted an invitation from my friend Warren Pease, the freelance journalist, to do a write-up on the growth of the panelized housing industry and the growth of Gilbilt. I hoped that somewhere some company might see it and be attracted to contact me. I was chumming the waters.

Gilbilt Homes, Inc. – Nashua, NH, 1969.
Bottom right – Gilbilt Village Display Park.
Center – Gilbilt's office.
Upper right – modular home factory.
Top center – materials storage.
Upper left – garage, cottage and panelized homes factory.

THE SELLOUT IN 1969 AND GILBILT HOMES BECOMES CONTINENTAL HOMES

T he concept of pre-fab homes had caught the fancy of Wall Street as it seemed to be the next logical way to satisfy the nation's housing shortage. I had planted some seeds and within a couple of months I was being wooed. First, a large company in Pittsburgh contacted me, then came United Artists. UA had just produced the "Endless Summer" a surfing movie and was rolling in cash. Why a movie production company wanted to buy me out was a bizarre concept and although it was flattering I turned their approach down even before an offering stage. Next, the giant insurance company CNA came after me. They were like a shark cruising the waters. The idea of being gobbled up was attractive but I just knew my still little company (in my eyes) would be lost in a shuffle of bureaucracy. CNA made increasingly attractive offers, but with each they created conditions I found distasteful. On the brink of a final agreement I rejected CNA and earned the ire of their contact person Lou Kane. I had known Lou from childhood days in Newton, Mass. He never spoke to me again, but he went on to open Au Bon Pain (the casual food and bakery chain) which company went national before he sold it.

It was just a few weeks later when my secretary Dolores Mooney laid an unopened envelope on my desk. It was marked personal with a postmark from Michigan City, Indiana. In his unsolicited letter Marvin Mitchell, the CEO of publicly traded conglomerate Weil-McLain, said he was looking to buy a company such as mine, and if I was interested to sell he would come to New

Hampshire to meet me. Apparently the article Warren Pease had published about Gilbilt's success was read even in Michigan City.

**Gilbilt Homes morphed into Continental Homes in 1970.
It commenced production of five homes a day, and never
looked back.**

THEN THINGS HAPPENED QUICKLY

O ut of the blue came Weil-McLain (stock symbol WMA). They were a small publicly held conglomerate from Michigan City, Indiana, and although publicly held it seemed to be operated like a family business. Weil-McLain's CEO visited me one time in Nashua. I was prepared and had several trucks washed and lined up for a few moments of visibility that morning. Each was loaded and the crews were ready to hit the road. I gave Marvin Mitchell the "deluxe" tour through the factory and introduced him to my secretary and every employee he stopped to observe. He seemed to be impressed and we got along instantly as if we were old friends.

Within a week Marvin called me and said he would like to buy Gilbilt and could I come to Michigan City, Indiana with my accountant. Did I need a push? Hardly. Three days later Arnold Edelstone and I were seated in Marvin's office, and within two hours a deal had been hammered out. Weil-McLain owned a variety of small to middle size companies in various manufacturing industries of which Weil-McLain boilers and Friedrich air- conditioners were the best known. Mine was to be the lead company in a division Marvin wanted to create of manufactured home companies throughout the East. I would head up that division. I didn't need a plane to fly back to Boston.

So, in late1969 I sold my company. I was given a substantial down payment with a payout to be executed in three years with interest to be paid quarterly on the outstanding balance, along with a generous monthly salary.

1969. Gilbilt is sold! Debbie planned and hosted the celebration party for friends and family. Left to right: Evi and Ezra Sheffres, Susan and Julie Gilman, Len and Debbie Gilman.

Most women enjoy planning a party, and some have that innate flair to carry it off with considerable élan. Debbie Gilman had that touch. Everything was "just right". To celebrate the sale of Gilbilt she booked a popular highway banquet restaurant and family and friends joined us. It was a joyous and memorable evening, particularly for those who had been involved from the beginning years of Gilbilt.

A few weeks later the company plane picked me up in Nashua. Marvin and I met in Chicago and from there we were scheduled to tour several small home fabricating companies in Indiana and Ohio. Together we had earmarked them as potential acquisitions. We hopped around and visited them, and at the end of the second day Marv left at South Bend and I was deposited at Chicago's O'Hare. As he left me that day he said, "Oh, by the way, you can congratulate me as tomorrow will be my 50'th birthday. I will be the first male member of my family to reach age 50 in several generations." Well you can guess what happened.

On my arrival back at Logan Airport in Boston I was being paged at the luggage pickup area. Bad news. Marv had fatally suffered a heart attack and died in South Bend an hour after I left him. **UNREAL!**

Still, the transition went relatively smoothly and Gilbilt was integrated with few, if any, bumps in the road. Except one; a major conflict with Marvin Mitchell's eventual successor.

It was not roses after Marvin died. One thing led to another – policy disagreements with Marvin's replacement CEO, and I left the company to retire to Florida in 1971, but I'm getting ahead of myself.

A FEW "GRAND" HELPED MAKE IT
A GRAND OPENING

In mid-summer 1970 with the help of my two Dolores' (my wife and my secretary, Dolores Johnson Mooney) we planned a factory grand opening which truly was grand. Invitees who attended were: United States Senator Norris Cotton, NH Governor Walter Peterson, Nashua Mayor "Dummy" Sullivan (his publicly referred to nickname), my good friend Attorney General Warren Rudman, many FHA officials, local bankers, the head designer from Slayter Associates, several dozen New England Building Inspectors, my parents, Boston media (including my friend Howard Flanagan from the Boston Globe who had been with me from the start, and helped me write my first garage ads so long ago), and quite a few friends and relatives. Everyone was seated beneath a huge white circus tent. A buffet luncheon was served followed by congratulatory speeches and predictions of how Gilbilt's modular homes would help meet the housing demand in New England, while also helping builders become 'year round business people'. Tours of the factory were sent off every few minutes.

It was a glorious, and even a sunny day; a day filled with pride and love for all those who had supported me from the time I first went to the Boston Public Library and read about how to build a one car garage. That day I gave bonuses to key people; Dolores Mooney, Larry Haiman, Sam Cresta, Bobby Westcott and Don Parker equal to a generous percentage of their annual salary. My accountant questioned me on the size of the total bonus package I gave away that day. I explained to him and many who had gawked at various overhead cranes, auto-nailers, truss presses, and assembly jigs, etc., that anyone could buy machinery but the greatest asset any company could have were its employees. I found myself repeating that thought several times that day. I truly believed it then and now.

P R O G R A M
CONTINENTAL HOMES DEDICATION CEREMONIES
Sunday, August 16, 1970
3 P. M. to 6 P. M.

PLANT TOUR — Guided tours of new plant to be conducted every 5 minutes from 3 o'clock to 4 o'clock.

TOUR OF MODEL HOME — First "Uni-structure" modular home built in Nashua Plant.

RIBBON CUTTING CEREMONY — 3:45 P. M.

SPEAKERS:

LEONARD GILMAN, President — Continental Homes, Inc.

DENNIS SULLIVAN, Mayor — City of Nashua

WALTER PETERSON, Governor — State of New Hampshire

NORRIS COTTON, U. S. Senator — State of New Hampshire

CHARLES KUHN, President — Weil McLain Co., Inc.
Michigan City, Indiana

JOHN SLAYTER, President — Slayter Associates, Inc.
Elkhart, Indiana

MODULAR HOME MANUFACTURING.

"THE GREAT TURN AROUND"

COCKTAILS   BUFFET SUPPER

CONTINENTAL HOMES OF NEW ENGLAND, INC.
Division of Weil-McLain Company, Inc.
Route 3, Daniel Webster Highway
Nashua, New Hampshire 03060

Three hundred Invitees were wined, dined and treated to tours through the first factory in the USA designed specifically for the manufacture of modular homes. Everything was perfect that day: the huge, white circus tent, the sunny sky, the drinks and food, the love. President Kuhn of Weil-McLain was a no-show.

The only hitch in the day's program was the new CEO of Weil-McLain was a no show. Weil-McLain's board of directors had just recently hired Charles Kuhn to be CEO. Kuhn was a hired gun from Texas and an off-putting one at that. He had been CEO of Dresser Industries. Dresser was, and is today, a huge company in the oil/energy business. Even then Dresser had several thousand employees. As a side investor Kuhn had been an investing founder of what became Southwest Airlines. I have always wondered about the circumstances which had Kuhn leaving Dresser for the smaller Weil-McLain. Perhaps his abrasive style rubbed Dresser's board of directors the wrong way. I can only say that I soon felt he may have had more prejudices than just being opposed to a modular home company in New Hampshire.

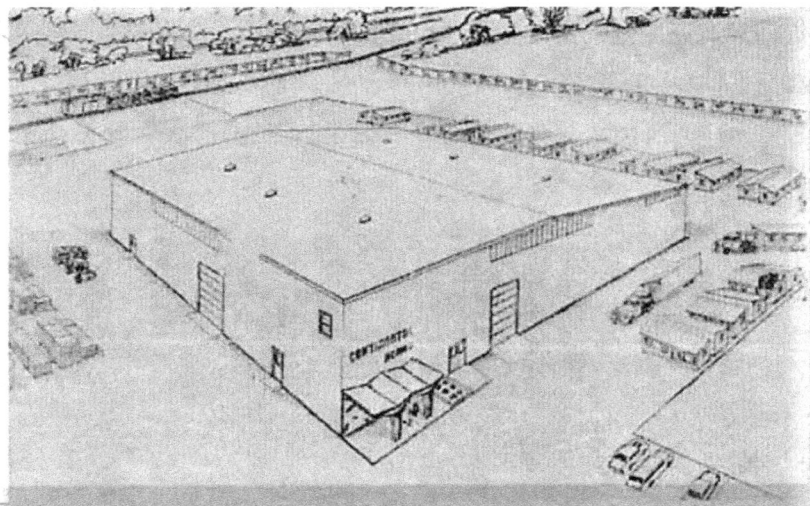

ARTIST'S RENDERING shows new Continental Homes plant which is now under construction in Nashua, New Hampshire. The facility will be used for the manufacture of modular homes. It has 89,000 square feet (about two acres) of manufacturing area plus 4,000 square feet of office space. To be completed by August, the plant will employ the most efficient techniques ever developed for building homes in a factory. It will have a one-shit capacity of five homes per day, and will be New England's largest and most modern facility for producing modular homes.

The Nashua Telegraph published a news story about Gilbilt changing its name to Continental and opening its new modular home factory. Comically it made a typo reporting on the factory having one-shiFt capacity of producing five homes a day.

Subsequent to the Grand Opening Texan Charles Kuhn did come to Nashua to tour the facility Weil-McLain now owned. It was at that first (and only) meeting in Nashua that he told me he despised companies in the construction field and that he disliked New England. Around the large oval table in our conference room I gathered eight of my key people to meet our new "boss". In fairness perhaps he was having a bad day, or was he showing his real colors when he became hostile to Ben Cohen, my soft spoken warehouse manager, who asked him if he was enjoying his tour through New England, and specifically here at Gilbilt? He responded, "Enjoyed? Enjoyed as compared to what?" A dropped pencil would have sounded like thunder. That was a conversation stopper and it was evident nothing would be further accomplished at this meeting. I tried to break the tension by saying how much everyone had enjoyed meeting him, and with that I adjourned the meeting. For Gilbilt's management team meeting Charles Kuhn was a morale downer.

Here are a few photos of the assembly line on which we built our modular homes.

Near station #3 of the assembly line.

Inside Continental's factory – the roller press for assembling roof trusses.

Assembly line in our modular homes factory.

Leonard Gilman

At the builder's site, Operation "Zip-up" takes place.

The two halves of the house, which always faced each other on the assembly line, meet again at the builder's site. There our two truck drivers, working with two of the builder's men, will roll the halves onto the full basement foundation where they are "mated" in what we called "Operation Zip-up." The following day a carpenter and helper, will complete the house. After the utilities are hooked up this home is ready for occupancy.

Somewhere in New England – a typical Continental modular home.

TINY BUBBLES

It was probably late 1970, and although I didn't know it at that time, my future with Gilbilt was uncertain. My company was just completing its first full year of shipping modular homes from its new factory in Nashua, NH. As the New England construction season was winding down I circulated a promotion to all my builder/dealers (particularly those in Maine, New Hampshire and Vermont). I communicated to them that now with our modular homes there was no need for a builder to go into self-imposed hibernation for the winter.

Here is what I proposed to our Builder/Dealers:

"If you will put in the foundations for five (5) homes before the ground freezes, we will ship your selected five modular homes on a staggered schedule in December, January, February and March. You will derive extra income. Income that in previous years you never generated, plus you will get a discounted percentage off the price schedule based on your current volume. In addition, I will send you and your wife (or significant other) on a ten day all-expense paid vacation to Hawaii!"

Best promo I ever ran! Twenty-two builders signed up. It benefitted everyone.

One of the benefits came as an unexpected surprise to me. The Boston travel agency I was working with for Hawaii arranged for Don Ho (Mr. "Tiny Bubbles") to perform on the stage of a Boston hotel for my builders and their wives as a lead up to their Hawaiian vacation.

That travel agency did a first class job! Prior to the show cocktails and hor d'oeuvres were served. It was a great, celebratory evening!

Sometime in January, 1971 I drove to Boston's Logan Airport to see my builder/dealers, their wives, and some of my key people off on their promised Hawaiian vacation. In addition to two of my shop foremen, I sent my sales manager, and my secretary along with their spouses on a well-deserved holiday vacation. Why didn't Len go? Len was going in another direction. I took my wife to St. Thomas and Jamaica where we lay on the beaches and I enjoyed my time away from business.

I had given my secretary money and a credit card and told her she would be the hostess for the Hawaiian trip. Yes, she took the entire group to see Don Ho perform and sing his famous "Tiny Bubbles" song. She told me about another night she took everyone to dinner at a restaurant which featured (unbeknown to her) totally nude waiters. When that trip was over how she would blush as she related how embarrassing it was to turn your head to the waiter to place your order and find yourself staring at his genitals at your eye level!

FAMILY

Throughout my business career there was one constant which enabled me to better enjoy my life – my employee "Family", and hopefully in return I was able to show my "Family" the rewards of honest work and honest dealing were more than accumulating wealth. Building relationships and memories were lasting. That "Family" – basically the key people who worked for me were the foundation which enabled Gilbilt to grow from a 100 SF office on "borrowed" land on the Revere Beach Parkway in Everett, Mass. to the most modern home assembly factory in the United States, covering almost two of the twenty acres of land it owned and occupied in Nashua, NH.

With fond memories and considerable nostalgia I humbly recall the REAL skilled, imaginative and loyal key employees and leaders: Bill Allen, Ray Beaudoin, Ben Cohen, Bob Collins, Normand Constant, Sam and Mario Cresta, Ray Demanche, Larry Haiman, Dolores Mooney Johnson, Paul Kidder, Jimmy Lawlor, Quentin Levesque, Bill Mayne, Eddie McLaughlin, Frankie Morin, Harriet O'Brien, Frank Orme, Frank Penney, Ray Sampson, Joe Silva, Ralph Simard, Gordon "Spike" Spicer, Bob and Pop Westcott, Rod Wright, and Joe Zarilla. I was fortunate that there exists in New Hampshire a genetic pool of craftsmen with a history of generations exhibiting an exceedingly high quality of workmanship combined with flawless character. Some call it "Yankee grit". I call it "Yankee pride". I apologize to those whose names I have overlooked.

Those people were the foundation of not just Gilbilt, but eventually several offshoot companies which followed. They were my

Team. Long ago I came across a quote by an unnamed author which goes, "No one can whistle a symphony, it takes a full orchestra to play it." Likewise, "Baseball cannot be properly played without a first-baseman." Those expressions define precisely how I always felt about the importance of my "team". Without my "team" Gilbilt never could have grown the way it did. My "team" were sometimes a little bit ahead of me, or else always at my side. They were never behind me, as we traveled down the road together. A team.

Sometime in 1971 Governor Walter Peterson honored me by appointing me to be one of the three New Hampshire Greyhound Racing Commissioners. We were charged with introducing that sport to New Hampshire. This entailed writing the Rules and Regulations, interviewing licensee applicants, and approving racetrack locations. I was appointed as Vice-Chairman. The Chairman was a purely political appointee and the Governor asked and advised me to please try to keep a leash on the Chairman and in particular his press releases. In discussion about this appointment with Weil-McLain one executive at the home office expressed his concerns. I reminded him I also had a life outside of Weil-McLain and assured him my personal life and interests would never interfere with my work. I was proud of that public service.

WINDING DOWN

The next, and last, time I met Charles Kuhn was at his office on State Street in Chicago in early 1971. His secretary had called me in Nashua the day before and said he would like to meet me the next day in Chicago. Walking into his office I had the feeling it was some kind of a setup. The only lettering on the glass front door was the suite number – no name. I had the feeling it could have been an office he had rented for the day (or possibly even by the hour).His secretary/receptionist (rent-a-person?) sat in a small room directly inside the office front door. She ushered me into Kuhn's office. He sat behind a desk devoid of everything except a few manila folders. The only other furniture was a plain wood chair. Does this sound like a movie set? Well, that thought occurred to me even then. Kuhn stared at me, twirled his glasses and told me that Marvin Mitchell's buying Gilbilt was a mistake, and if I expected to be paid out in a timely manner that my company would have to generate all the money that Weil-McLain owed me. He emphasized to me how he always believed in going "First Class", and that Mitchell had stooped below that bar when he bought Gilbilt. That, plus being a Texas man he had no interest in a New England company. If Marvin Mitchell were alive, I doubt he would have hired Charles Kuhn.

Then, he dismissed me. I couldn't believe it. He had me schlep to Chicago just to tell me off, and dismiss me ...all in less than fifteen minutes. We did not shake hands when I left. As I went down in the elevator I felt like I was dropping into an abyss. Kuhn's last words ringing in my ears.....something about "traveling First Class." I went to a pay phone and called my wife...told her to pack and make plans for a vacation to start in two days. At O'Hare, with a smile, I changed my flight back to Nashua to a 'first class' seat. Debbie and I left for Florida two days later. I finished out the fiscal year remaining on my contract and left the company. I was paid out per my contract on my last day as originally scheduled. I was pleased knowing that on a percentage basis (net to sales revenues) Gilbilt ranked near the top of all of Weil-McLain's companies.

EPILOGUE

I n later years I enjoyed hearing of the enterprising successes of former employees Ray Beaudoin, Mario Cresta, and Eddie McLaughlin, all of whom went on to operate their own successful businesses. I spoke with my "hipster" yard foreman George Labonte who had become a building inspector. Larry Haiman, Gilbilt's long time Sales Manager went on to be President of Keyloc, a newly started modular home manufacturer. Larry spoke graciously of me at Sam Cresta's retirement dinner which was attended by most everyone in the Northeast factory-built housing industry. Almost all at one time or another, had initially worked for me at Gilbilt. I was sent a tape of that dinner meeting and I watched Larry saying, "....few of us would be here today if it wasn't for 'the little guy' who had the guts to start it all."

At a luncheon reunion in Burlington, Mass. in 2005 my wife and I met with Bob Killkelly (Bob had replaced Larry Haiman as sales manager), Sam Cresta, my first secretary Barbara Ferson, one of our first modular truck drivers Frank Penney, and Don Parker's wife Jeanne. I loved Sam Cresta like a brother and I know he felt the same about me. We hugged and wept together as we said our goodbyes.

Dick "Eggs" O'Brien died after fighting cancer for years. His wife Harriet, my secretary for years, read my condolence letter at his funeral. Don Parker died of a stroke in 2001. He never adjusted to the new owners of the company. I flew to Boston and visited Pop Westcott in the Leahy clinic shortly before he died. Sam Tamposi, Mario Vagge, Marvin Gould and Larry Haiman are all long gone. Bobby Westcott died suddenly from a medication reaction. I exchange e-mails with his son occasionally. Gone also are my two accountants; Barney

Yanofsky and Arnold Edelstein. Gilbilt/Continental was sold and resold several times before the factory was torn down and it became the site of the Pheasant Lane Mall, one of the largest in New Hampshire. Vic Charpentier passed away before his famous and beloved Green Ridge Turkey Farm Restaurant was sold and subsequently torn down. I communicate occasionally with Don Parker's daughters, Warren Rudman's daughter, and now pleasantly Paul Kidder's daughter. It is gratifying when some employees mentioned in this remembrance, call me out of the blue. Why not? After all they're "family".

Sam Cresta and Len Gilman had a joyful reunion in 2005. We laughed at reminiscences, and sobbed as we said goodbye. We were like brothers. It would be the last time we would meet.

GILBILT CHRONOLOGY

- 1955 – Gilman Garage Co. started at 79 Milk Street, Boston
- !956 -1957 Gilbilt Garage Co. on Revere Beach Parkway, Everett, Mass.
- 1958 – 1962 Gilbilt Lumber Co. on Route 3A in Burlington, Mass.
- 1962 – 1969 Gilbilt Homes, Co. on Route 3 Bypass in Nashua, NH
- 1969 – Gilbilt sold to Weil-McLain, is re-named Continental Homes
- 1970 – Grand Opening of the modular homes factory in Nashua
- 1971 – Len retired from Continental Homes
- 1972 – Len moved to Florida

REMINISCING – GILBILT FIRSTS

- The first company in New England advertising factory built garages and installing them on-site.

- The first company in New England offering and installing factory built vacation homes. The first company (perhaps in the United States) to use stapling hammers and then automatic-nailers in the factory and on site.

- The first company in New England to offer panelized homes to the public.

- The first company in New England to offer factory built homes with roof trusses.

- The first company in the United States to manufacture modular homes in a factory specifically designed for that purpose.

WITH GRATITUDE

I thank my daughter Julie, and friends Amy and Bill for their efforts to edit and make sense of my aberrant, grammar and punctuation disasters. Please contact them regarding any missing commas or dangling participles. I thank my dear friends Marcia and Jack for inspiring me to put my story to print and smoothing some rough edges. Last, but hardly least, a big hoorah for Dan, my computer maven, who brought many of the photographs into sharper focus.

I dedicate this nostalgic remembrance to Debbie Gilman. She traveled every mile of the road with me.

As I said on Page One, I started on the road of my journey, as described, when I was 26. That was 65 years ago. I am grateful for the long and fortunate life I have enjoyed. In everything we accomplish, there is always a certain "element of luck" involved. Beyond luck, there is only one's self-determination, and the input and participation of others. Throughout my story I have named many people. I know there were times when each of them gave me a lift by guiding and helping me travel "Len's Road". I thank every one of them.

Yes, as Robert Frost wrote: Len's Road was "The Road Not Taken".

"Two roads diverged in a wood, and I—I took the one less traveled by, And that has made all the difference."

–Robert Frost

Leonard Gilman

Those were some great years!

Thanks for the memories.

You know who you are – I want my half of the ping-pong table back. ☺

—Len Gilman, 2020

CPSIA information can be obtained
at www.ICGtesting.com
Printed in the USA
BVHW011801110920
588626BV00002B/11